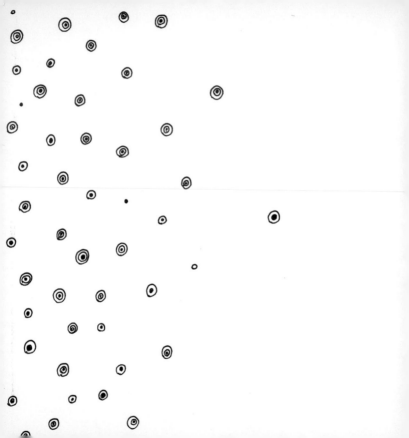

To: _____

From: _____

Date: _____

# Handwritten Notes to My Friend

**HARVEST HOUSE PUBLISHERS**

EUGENE, OREGON

Produced and originated by PQ Blackwell Limited

forever

Besties
are
forever

I have spent some of
the happiest moments
of my life with you.
... I love being friends
with you.

HERE'S A
BIG HUG
FROM ME, TO
SHOW I CARE
AND YOU'RE IN
MY THOUGHTS
EVEN WHEN
I CAN'T BE THERE

XO

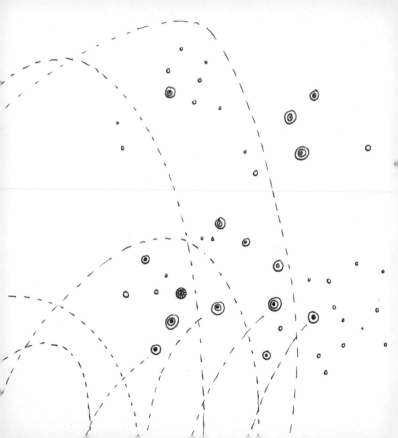

Remember
the path is not straight
mistakes need not be fatal

Whenever I finish a good book,
I immediately want to take it over
to your house and demand that you
read it on the spot so we can discuss it
in great detail.

Your opinion means so much to me

BEING YOUR FRIEND IS EXCITING.
YOU EMBRACE LIFE WITH SO MUCH ENTHUSIASM
AND ARE ALWAYS UP FOR ANYTHING NO MATTER WHAT.
TELL ME, DO YOU EVER RUN OUT OF ENERGY,
OR DO YOU POSSESS SOME KIND
OF SUPERPOWER?

I overheard some people talking about you the other day. They were talking about what a unique and interesting person you are, how you're so warm and friendly and always make people feel good about themselves. I agree with them.

May the Lord keep watch
between you and me when
we are away from each other.

— The Book of Genesis

Wherever we go
and whatever life sends
I know we'll always be
the BEST of FRIENDS

# YAY
## FOR BEING BEST FRIENDS WITH YOU

DO YOU KNOW THAT NOT ONLY IS
YOUR PRESENCE HUGELY IMPORTANT
TO ME, BUT THAT THE UNIVERSE
WOULD BE UNDER SERIOUS THREAT
IF YOU WEREN'T AROUND?
IN FACT, I HAVE HEARD THAT
YOUR EXISTENCE IS CRUCIAL TO THE
SURVIVAL OF SEVERAL RARE SPECIES.

YOU'RE THE BEE'S KNEES
(BEES HAVE AMAZING KNEES)

A sweet friendship
refreshes the soul.

— The Book of Proverbs

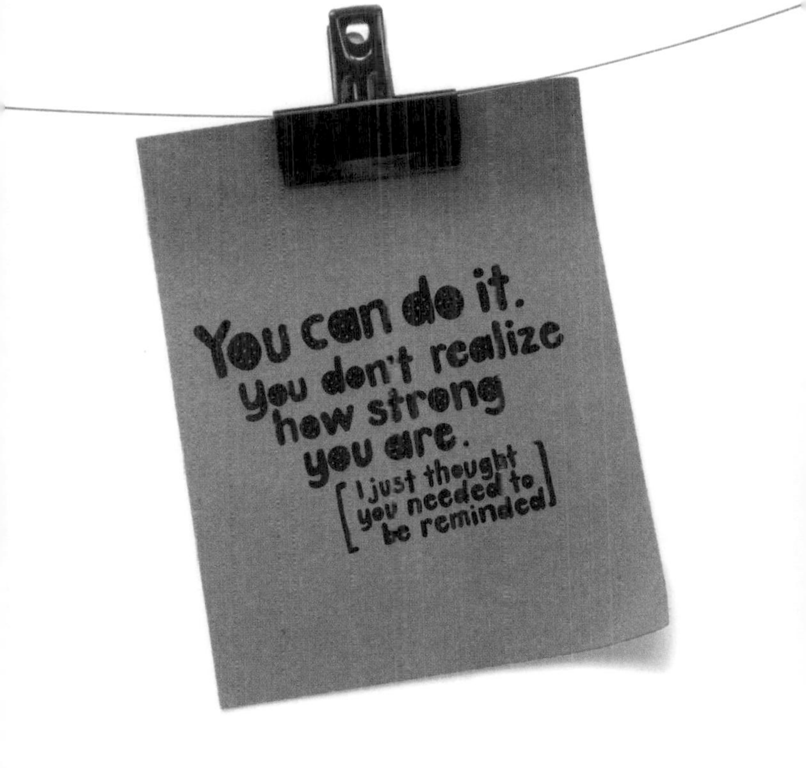
You can do it.
You don't realize
how strong
you are.
[I just thought
you needed to
be reminded]

I am Your
FRIEND

I am Your friend ...☺

(:

I am your friend

I am
your
friend :)

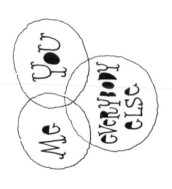

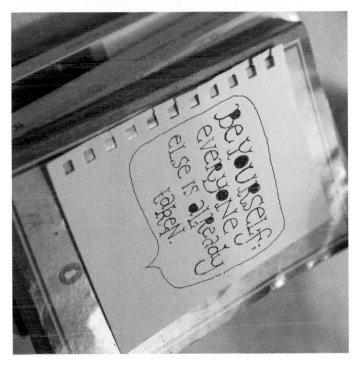

# THANKS

...FOR reminding me that the world is a wonderful place with so much fun to be had.

I couldn't stop thanking God for you—every time I prayed, I'd think of you and give thanks.

—The Book of Ephesians

You are cordially invited on an adventure with me.

WHERE SHALL WE GO AND WHAT SHALL WE DO? WRITE BACK SOON.

YOU'RE A TRUE FRIEND.
HOW MANY TIMES HAVE YOU LISTENED
TO ME POUR MY HEART OUT TO YOU?
YOU'RE ALWAYS THERE FOR ME.
I'M SO GRATEFUL FOR THAT.
ALL MY LOVE...AND MELODRAMA—
YOUR FRIENDSHIP IS SUCH A COMFORT TO ME.

MY DEAR FRIEND

THINKING OF YOU

I SAW A
RAINBOW
TODAY, AND
IT REMINDED
ME OF YOU,
A COLORFUL
CONTRIBUTION
TO THE WORLD.

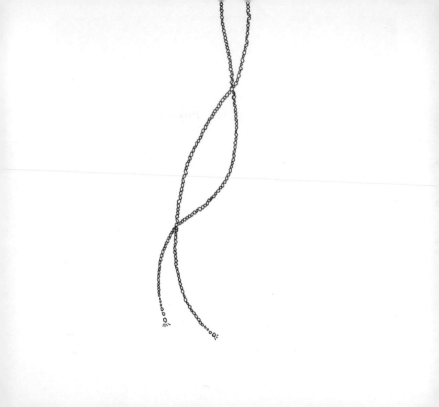

Many People
will walk in and out
of your life but only
true friends will
leave footprints
in your
heart.

A WALK THROUGH THE WOODS
WITH YOU ON A SUNNY DAY
IS THE PERFECT TONIC
FOR MY SPIRITS.
SO PUT ON YOUR SENSIBLE
WALKING SHOES
AND JOIN ME.

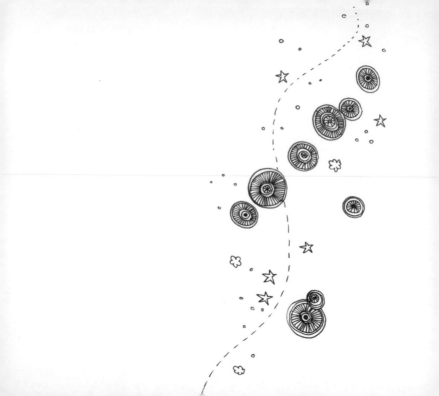

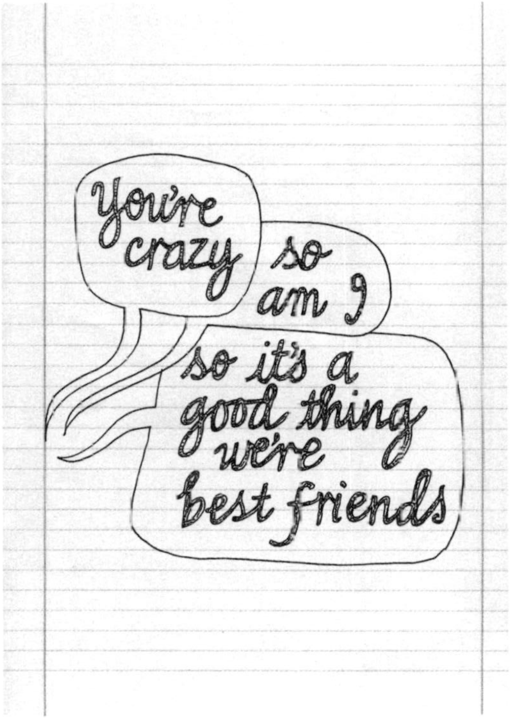

You're crazy
so am I
so it's a good thing we're best friends

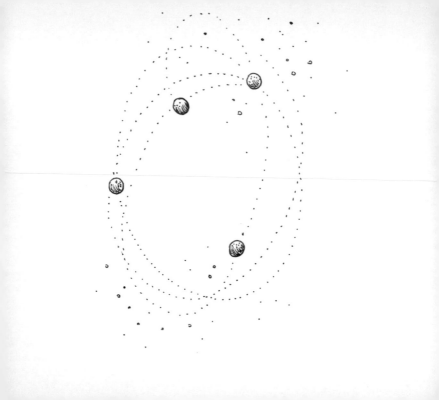

if I ever get asked
to lead a space voyage
to the moon, I promise
that I will take you
with me. In the meantime,
we can sit on the roof
and gaze at the stars.

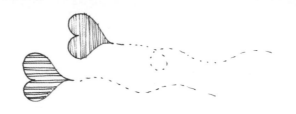

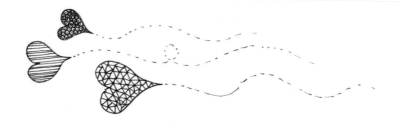

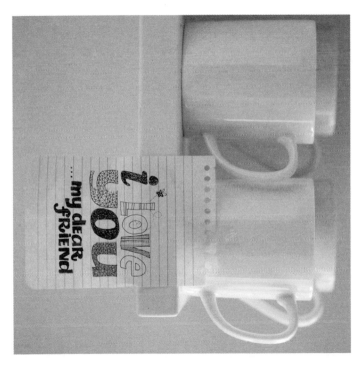

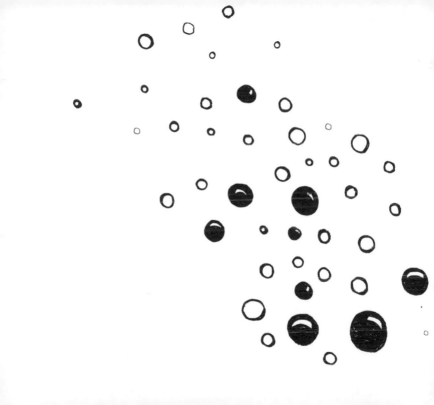

I'M WRITING TO INFORM YOU
THAT WE ARE NOW OVERDUE
FOR A LONG CHAT.
I HAVE SO MUCH TO TELL YOU...

the other day
   on the street I passed
   2 girls laughing
with abandon, and it
   reminded me of us.
(of course they were wearing good shoes...)

A friend loves at all times.

-The Book of Proverbs.

**Handwritten Notes to My Friend**

Concept, design, text, images copyright © 2011 by PQ Blackwell Limited. All worldwide rights reserved.
www.pqblackwell.com

Produced and originated by PQ Blackwell Limited
116 Symonds Street, Auckland, New Zealand
www.pqblackwell.com

Published by Harvest House Publishers
Eugene, Oregon 97402
www.harvesthousepublishers.com

ISBN 978-0-7369-4570-7

Illustrations by Carla Shale
Quote research and creation by Rachel Clare
Book design by Cameron Gibb and Sarah Anderson
Photograph acknowledgements are as follows: pp. 9, 15, 23, 27, 35, 43, 47, 51, 57 and 63 by Jacqui Blanchard; pp. 5, 11, 13, 16, 19, 24–25, 31, 32–33, 39, 48–49 and 52 by Carla Shale; front and back cover and pp. 6, 7, 10, 17, 36, 37, 40, 41, 45, 53, 55, 58, 60 and 61 by iStockphoto; pp. 28–29 by PQ Blackwell.

Scripture quotations are taken from the Holy Bible, *New International Version*®, NIV®. Copyright © 1973, 1978, 1984, 2011 by Biblica, Inc. ™ Used by permission. All rights reserved worldwide; *The Message*. Copyright © by Eugene H. Peterson 1993, 1994, 1995, 1996, 2000, 2001, 2002. Used by permission of Navpress Publishing Group; and *The Living Bible*, Copyright © 1971, Used by permission of Tyndale House Publishers, Inc, Wheaton, IL 60189 USA. All rights reserved.

The publisher has made every effort to trace the ownership of all poems and quotes. In the event of a question arising from the use of a poem or quote, we regret any error made and will be pleased to make the necessary correction in future editions of this book.

'The path is not straight. Mistakes need not be fatal' used with permission of Marion Winik.

**Printed in China**

12 13 14 15 16 17 18 19 / LP / 10 9 8 7 6 5 4 3 2 1

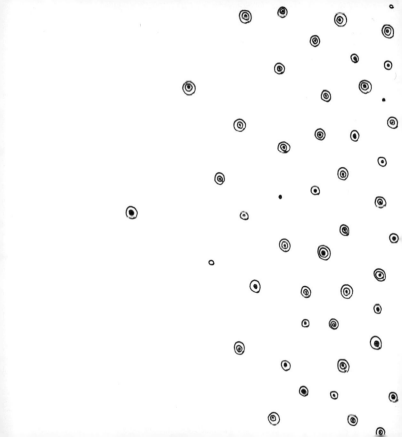

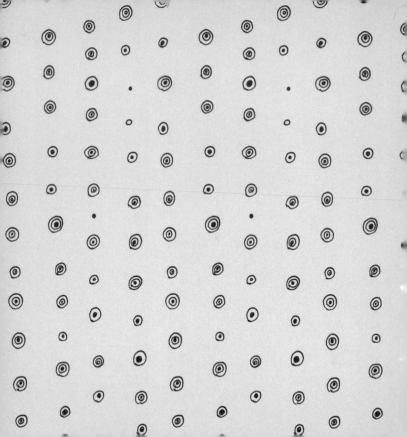